The Weddin

LINDA CHASE grew up in a suburb of New York City and studied creative writing at Bennington College in Vermont. She worked as a stage costume designer in San Francisco and later in Edinburgh, where her children were born and where she began studying Tai Chi. In 1980 she moved to Manchester and established her own Tai Chi school while continuing to write, teach and publish poetry. She teaches at the Arden School of Theatre in Manchester and is the founding chairperson of the Forum for Tai Chi and Special Needs. Her previous collections include the pamphlet *Young Men Dancing* (Smith/Doorstop, 1993) and *These Goodbyes* (Fatchance, 1995). Her poems have won many prizes and appeared widely in magazines.

Also by Linda Chase

Young Men Dancing
These Goodbyes

LINDA CHASE

The Wedding Spy

CARCANET

First published in Great Britain in 2001 by
Carcanet Press Limited
4th Floor, Conavon Court
12–16 Blackfriars Street
Manchester M3 5BQ

A CIP catalogue record for this book
is available from the British Library

ISBN 1 85754 556 7

The publisher acknowledges financial assistance
from the Arts Council of England

Set in Monotype Ehrhardt by XL Publishing Services, Tiverton
Printed and bound in England by SRP Ltd, Exeter

for Andrew

Acknowledgements

Thanks are due to the editors of the following journals, in which some of these poems appeared:

Ambit; *Envoi*; *Frogmore Papers*; *Orbis*; *Peterloo Competition Anthology*; *PN Review*; *Tai Chi*; *The New Writer*; *The North*; *The Rialto*; *Wide Skirt*.

'What to Do with Sorrow' won First Prize in the Dulwich Poetry Competition. 'Resting Place' won Second Prize in the Cardiff International Poetry Competition.

Contents

I

II

III

I

Manhasset Saturday

1. The Chinese Laundry

Not the actual shirts, in detail,
but she remembers their packaging,
wrapped in flimsy brown paper
folded carefully without any tape,
then looped with thin white string,
two ways round and tied
on top with a single bow.

The shirts were folded carefully
half way along each shoulder,
turning the bodice in to the middle.
Yes, she could picture them.
The sleeves were smoothed out,
laid down the length of the back,
the tail flipped up, body turned down.
Even thirds were creased into the shirt,
held in place by a band of light blue paper,
the width of three of her fingers.
The package itself could easily bend
but a week's worth of shirts made it firmer.

Light starch on the collars and cuffs
her mother said each time she left
a bundle of soiled shirts on the counter.
L44 had been penned already by hand
inside every one of the collars.
The girl had seen them do it,
stretching the fabric across a wooden disk,
held in place by a wooden hoop.
'Why didn't they use Chinese numbers?'
she remembers wondering at the time.
Maybe no one would have trusted them.

Her father's shirts were fine Egyptian cotton.
The details were coming back to her –
how they were made to measure,
had tiny monograms hand-stitched on the fronts.
Sometimes white on white, so subtle
that the letters actually couldn't be seen.
Did the shirtmaker think of this,
she wondered, or was it her father's idea?

In the front of the shop,
a Chinese woman ironed by hand,
hour after hour and next to her,
another woman used a giant press for sheets.
Steam and starch filled the shop front
with a mist as pure as baptism –
a purging that could go as deep as bones.
Cleanliness had never smelled as pure
as it did in the front of the Chinese laundry.

But that Saturday morning,
when she showed the owner
the folded slip of pink paper,
he beckoned her with his index finger
to come to the back of the shop with him
to look for her father's shirts
among the racks of stacked up packages.
The pink-slipped ones were on one shelf
and other colours had shelves of their own.

Another man was there, just standing.
He spoke Chinese to the owner.
Then the owner said in English
(he must have wanted her to understand)
'Isn't she a pretty girl?'
but the other man answered in Chinese.

Then without speaking,
the owner opened his palm
and spread his hand
across her tender forming
breast and squeezed it,
wrinkling the freshly ironed
cotton of her blue and white
checked cowgirl shirt.
Then he moved his hand
to her other breast,
bunching the shirt
and squeezing again.

The other man laughed,
then both men spoke Chinese,
back and forth rapidly.
She could hear the steam of the iron,
the clamping sound of the giant press
coming from the front of the shop
where the women were speaking Chinese.

One woman ironed by hand,
another used the giant press for sheets.
Steam and starch filled the shop front with mist.

2. Wright's Hardware Store

She hadn't given it another thought –
not even when she met her father
in Wright's Hardware Store,
their favourite stop on Saturday mornings,
because he hadn't thought of it either.
She wasn't carrying a package of shirts.

'Oh, Princess, you surprised me!'
her father said when she came up behind him
and whispered 'boo' directly into his ear.
He was holding a two-handed plane
and miming the action of planing.
It had been her idea in the first place.

A plane could even off the strips of wood
wedged in the gaps of his work bench.
He had tapped them in with a mallet
to fill the spaces left between the planks –
a remedy for disappearing screws and nails
which fell between the cracks.

She had helped him at every stage –
holding the ends of the heavy planks,
walking them forward slowly
as he fed them into the circular saw.
To his surprise, she even helped him
choose the tool for the final job.

At home, her mother asked about the shirts,
but the daughter had nothing to say.
Instead, she talked about selecting tools
for tomorrow's woodwork strategy.
The Chinese laundry had vanished in steam
and the man's hands had never touched her.

Her father's shirts, bleached out, white,
abandoned on the counter, left behind.
'Don't worry, Sugar,' her mother said,
'we'll pick them up on the way to the beach.
I'm sure your purse is still there, too.'
But the girl didn't hear what she said.

On Sunday she would help her father
sweep up the curls of wood his plane
had pared away from the uneven top.
Quick strokes, catching and slicing,
shaping the surface of the bench into
how it should have been from the beginning.

3. Beach Outing

The child says no.
Everyone in the car hears her.
No. She will not get out.
She will not go into the Chinese laundry.
She will not obey in the way
a good daughter is meant to obey.

Being good hadn't helped anyway.
All day being good and at night,
just some idle exploring at first
and then her hands found a purpose,
pinching her own tender nipples
for the sweetness of pain letting go.

His touch had not been sweet
although he had asked her nicely
to follow him behind the racks of shirts.
She will not get out of the car.
No one in the car knows why
the child says no.

She couldn't stop thinking of angels
in the snow each time
the temperature dropped
and the sky turned grey.

Will it snow today?
Please let it snow today and let
the snow be unbearably sentimental
like icing sugar spread on gingerbread.

When the flakes finally fell and settled,
she instructed the young man to place
her chair in front of the window.
'Open it,' she said, 'and leave me.'

As swiftly as the blast of cold
entered the room and chilled her face,
a pair of children appeared outside.
They held hands and looked up at her.

The small girl, angelic in her turquoise
one-piece snowsuit, stepped across
the unmarked snow to the middle of the lawn.
She lay down on her back and fanned her arms.

The boy, much older, watched carefully
as if learning a new skill. He followed
in her tracks and stood at her feet.
He lay down, a mirror, an echo of rustling feathers.

Dream Car

In the Oldsmobile of my dreams
I pick you up.

It is black and heavy as a tank,
though relieved by rusting chrome
which gleams in spite of itself.

It is more like a scoop
with an open mouth –
remember the oval lips
of a 49 Olds?

You are running down the street,
afraid to look around when I beep the horn.

You keep on running down the next block
and lose me when I have to stop
for traffic and lights
and people crossing the road.

You keep to your side of the street,
block after block. Nothing stops you
but your child's heart finally
running out of breath.

My heavy door swings out
in front of you.
Panting and gasping,
you scramble in.

The leather seats amaze you.
The silver buttons catch your eye
and you push them down, first one
and then the other, to lock yourself in.

It happens so fast, that change.
The fear of getting in
and the wish to stay inside.

Friends of my Parents

The Fairmont Hotel has parking in the basement
so I knew I wouldn't be late. But first,
I had to find some tights without a run.

And a dressy dress. Get there, drive in and park.
Elevator to the top and meet them in the bar.
Take cash for the parking, cigarettes, Tampax.

Linny, sweetheart, order whatever you want.
Paté, lobster, chocolate mousse, a Napa Valley wine,
strong espresso coffee, San Francisco style.

The food is great when friends of my parents
come to town and call me from fancy hotels.
Waiters, doormen and the latest hometown news.

No, no, said Fred, in the middle of a story,
it wasn't Sally. It was one of her father's girlfriends.
You remember, that tall skinny young one.

Josie kicked her husband hard under the table.
She had to slump in her chair to reach him.
Don't kick me, Josie, he said. Come on,

Linny knows about her father's girlfriends.
He seemed so sure at first, then later, not so sure.
You do know, Linny, don't you?

Of course I know.
Everyone knows what my father is like.
The waiter asked me twice if I wanted sugar.

But I could see my mother, in her golf dress,
standing in our Johnny Appleseed kitchen,
the wallpaper fresh with apples and trees.

She slammed down the phone. A Martini,
I think, in those days was in her other hand.
Let's eat, kids. Your father isn't coming home.

Fred came down to the basement with me
and paid for parking my car.
I could see him waving in my rear view mirror.

Through the windscreen, the streets of Nob Hill
were steaming with the first autumn rain.
I could see the lights across the Bay

until the nose of my car took a dive.
My night on the town had been cheap.
I wasn't even a nickel down.

Frisco

He had one of those plain American names
like Jim. Pink skin, a little raw from shaving.
Bristles on the neck. Soft, blond, boyish ones.
Maybe it was Tom. He wasn't shy.
Tip-toeing from the bath to the bed
he held the towel out in his hand.
He dried his neck and grinned.

San Francisco, full of orange and yellow nasturtiums,
eucalyptus trees, red wine, hamburgers and art.
Cats, beads, espresso coffee on Haight Street.
He wouldn't be seeing any of this.
Jack was a soldier, not a tourist.
He hadn't come to Frisco for flowers or peace.
He called it Frisco, the way mid-westerners did,
not really knowing the reason why.
Old movies, I guess. Shipping out from Frisco.

But flying was so different.
It happened fast. I asked him on the plane.
An ordinary United Airlines flight.
I got on in New York. He got on in Chicago.
I just asked him, not beating around the bush.
Did he want to? He did.

I knew I would hold him all night
and do all the things an eighteen-year-old boy
dreams an older girl might do to him.
It was a war movie, before battle.
Bob was his name. I held him all night.
I slid my tongue into cracks.
I let my fingers go everywhere.
I opened my body. I guided him in
with my hand. This way. Come this way.
It was a very warm night.
There mustn't have been any fog.
It smelled like lemon groves
three hundred miles away in the San Fernando Valley.

Pete was his name, I remember now.
I drove him to the airport in the morning.
All I could say was goodbye.
The war took two more years.
It took me thirty years to remember as much as this.

Photo Journal by Paul Fusco

(Robert F. Kennedy 1925 to 1968)

When the train came out of the tunnel
from New York, it went all the way to Virginia
and all along the way, Americans stood
beside the tracks, planted firmly, waiting.

Young boys, at attention, had no shirts.
Fat women sat in convertibles and families
lined up according to size and rank
to watch the funeral train pass.

They couldn't see the coffin
or the flag or any bullet holes
but they were satisfied to stand
and hold their right hands on their hearts.

The photographer said that from this day on
the country began to fall apart.
The girl in the bright pink two-piece
bathing-suit had no idea if this would be true.

She stood alone at the edge of a field.
The truth came later. When the train came out
of the tunnel from New York, it went all the way
to Virginia. Virginia. Then whistle stops.

Gino's

We snuck in here with fake ID
when we were only 17 –
a local bar in any suburb of New York
but it happened to be ours.

'Why not meet where the memories are?'
he said to me on the phone.
'We can go to the hospital later.
Just get a cab from JFK.'

No one remembers us here.
He wonders if the bartender is the son
of the bartender we used to know
but we decide not to ask.

Our mother is dying
and we are afraid to look each other in the eye,
but we do because she is dying
and we have so little time.

My brother says, out loud, he loves me.
I hate this news, coming so late,
remembering myself, little girl with pig-tails
aching to be in the big boys' gang.

Love, out loud, would have been enough
to let that little girl sleep late on Saturdays
with her favourite stuffed animal under her chin
instead of going out to look for turtles.

It would have been enough, later
to let her wear makeup and high heeled shoes
and enjoy the wonders of underwear
encasing her changing body.

Even later, it would have been enough
to let her keep her boyfriends hungry
for orgasms, cigarettes, Scotch and forgiveness.
My brother says he always loved me.

Our mother is dying
and we are afraid to look each other in the eye,
but we do because she is dying
and this is the time we've got.

My Brother and the Moon

'If my sister wants to call me, collect,
from the fucking moon, I'll take the call.'
It was only from Boston, though.
Boston to Vermont doesn't cost much.

One of those snow and fog nights with
all the planes grounded at Christmas
and the airport heaving like a refugee camp.
Our plane from LA was the last one in.

The kids and I, sitting on our luggage,
counting out quarters, nickels and dimes.
The change went on chocolate chip cookies,
the only food left for sale.

Midnight in Vermont, finally in the car,
chains slapping the road, but holding us,
he told me what he had said to his wife,
not what she had said to him first.

I've had years and years to wonder
what it was and I think it wasn't nice.
I prefer to think about my brother and the moon
and other collect calls I still might make.

The Wedding Spy

I went to your son's wedding today
in a carefully chosen outfit.
I wore the kind of dress
an aunt of the groom is supposed to wear,
but I think it was a bit too long.
I had a hat, which slipped slightly
onto my left eyebrow.
I wore brick coloured sandals with straps.

I kissed the people whose lips moved,
shook hands when a hand was extended.
I sat where I saw my name on a card
and spoke only of family connections.
'The groom is my nephew,'
I said to the mother of the bride.
She was happy enough with that,
scanning my face for resemblance.

People talked to me, remembering you
and I remembered you too.
In fact, as they spoke, I thought I was you,
being me, in a mint cotton dress,
a straw hat and brick coloured shoes.
I wore jewellery and stayed at a proper hotel.
Anyone could have reached me there
but later no one phoned.

Remember the yarmulkes,
the chuppa, the Hebrew prayers?
The Rockies, the sun, the Colorado jays?
I stayed a spy as long as I could
without slipping or losing myself
in the accents and outfits forever.
You would have fitted in better.
I wish you had impersonated yourself.

Cornus Collection

My mother's old gold jewellery looked like
these bracts with tightly rolled brown-gold balls
pinned to the centre of each creamy palm.
I call the trees themselves 'My Cornus Collection'
to keep casual admirers at arm's length.

I avoid the word 'dogwood' because it's familiar.
People imagine they know what it means.
Visitors, strolling, nod their heads and point,
'Oh yes,' they say, 'a dogwood tree.'
because they heard once of red stems in winter.

On Long Island, the dogwood tree was mine
and my brother had the huge sugar maple.
We shared the white oak in the back yard
because it was big enough for both of us to sit in,
reading comics and telling knock-knock jokes.

My dogwood was pink in the spring and fragile.
Climbing it was always out of the question,
but my brother let me clamber through his maple
in the summer and hang from low branches
by my hooked-over, blue-jeaned knees.

Now, in England I have an old cedar tree
which the cats climb up to hide from the dog.
I have chestnuts, limes, sycamores, hawthorns.
Beside these trees, I've planted my young cornuses –
exotic and unique. I walk among them saying,

'Darling American cornuses,' and the litany begins,
'*Cornus kousa* Madame Butterfly, *Cornus kousa chinensis*,
Cornus florida Princess, *Cornus nuttallii*,
Cornus nuttallii Ormonde,' because I'm sure
whoever listens will have no idea what I mean.

Doodle Dandy

Because I'm rather wise and far too old
for mini skirts and two piece bathing suits
I keep myself in England where it's cold.

The rain is helpful too. The moss and mould
have been allowed to settle on my boots
because I'm rather wise and far too old.

I thought I liked the look of weathered gold,
the wilting sound of madrigals and lutes
so here I am in England where it's cold.

But I was wrong – America unfolds
her glitz and kitsch. Her honky-tonk pollutes
the part of me that's wise and far too old.

I'm uncontrolled, now sillier and bold
enough to score yet stay in good repute –
Fuck England and decorum. Fuck the cold.

Fuck youth. I'm having my opinions polled.
I'm taking back my accent and my roots.
I'm finally wise enough and far too old
to stay on here in England where it's cold.

Me, Instead of Arthur Miller

Didn't you come to see *me*, instead of Arthur Miller?
I had seen the first act already — Biff and Hap on stage,
caught up in lies. Willie was working on commission,
driving his car from Brooklyn to Boston just to see
his bit-on-the-side in nylons. He wasn't making sales.

At the interval, weaving your smile through the crowd
I saw you coming my way and called out 'Darling! Darling!
Wonderful to see you. How did you know I was here?'
'I didn't,' you said. 'I came to see the play. Linda *Loman*
was the one I came to see and Willie and her two boys.'

I couldn't argue with you about it since you had tickets
and seats and friends to sit with and it was clear to me
you had seen the first act and planned to see more. You,
my English son, sitting through the all-American play
of all time, wondering how they got the accents wrong.

You could have grown up with this play, spoken perfectly,
staged with real footballs, real polluted air, real dreams
of success rising above the embattlement of Ebbets Field.
And when your heart was due to break, it might have
shattered in the all-American way with a Brooklyn accent.

My friends and I are watching from the other side
of the theatre and we know most of the lines by heart.
We know that act two will follow act one and that
the outcome was decided before you, my son, were born —
you who have never made a touch-down in your life.

I think that Arthur Miller went too far at the end,
having Willie plant the vegetable seeds in the dark.
'I have nothing in the ground,' he says, while digging,
having to put the flashlight down to open the envelope,
Linda and the two sons, completely powerless to stop him.

II

Dear Disciple

Give me the focus of your eyes and don't blink.
Give me all the love in your heart.
Give me your money.

Give me your weekends and your days off.
Give me all the minutes in every hour.
Give me your sleep.

Give me your books, your CDs and your computer.
Give me all your software.
Give me your room.

Give me your restless nights in tangled sheets.
Give me all your longing for touch.
Give me your celibacy.

Give me a cut in your skin and spread the edges out.
Let it be deep, gushing with blood.
I want to slip the message in.

Is this too much to ask?

Arriving Late for the Secret of Life

Arriving late for the secret of life
has caused you deep uncertainty.
You can never be sure, really sure,
what the first sentence actually was.

It could have begun:
'*Only a fool would think*', or
'*the opposite to this follows and is true*', or
'*if you believe this, you are doomed to burn in hell*', or
'*only after fasting for six months,
could a mortal begin to understand*'.

So, when you came in late,
after I had already written down
all of the sentences given,
I noticed you catching my eye
and I saw how your eyebrow raised
in the manner of asking a question.
You knew that I knew how the secret begins.

You came to me from across the room
and you sat on the floor cross-legged
and you've stayed by my side ever since.

Daily Practice

Was it you who made the tea in the yellow pot
and lit the Chinese incense before I came downstairs?
You and fresh flowers, arranged in front of me.

We sit cross-legged through this unfolding hour,
held by long, sweet in-breaths before the traffic stirs,
stopping and starting our minds with lists of things to do.

All day we vie with our computers, scanners, phones
and bounce around within our carnival of screens
reading messages – these tiny bits of text that bind.

You mustn't tell anyone I've cooked for you tonight.
These are secret bowls of food we eat with chop-sticks
behind the jasmine trellis when the sun goes down.

Come here. Our final practice time is in the dark.
I find you by touch and stick to you all night,
though I know you don't know how dark it can get.

You could have been surprised by this waking up,
not knowing where in the world this new place is.
It is black and blacker. It is light and lighter.

Resting Place

In case there is any doubt
about where would be a good place
to rest your hand for the night,
I shall tell you. My belly is it.

Try it. It's just the right shape
to let your hand cup at the fingers.
Your palm doesn't even have to stretch
to feel the softness churning with power.

Rest. Even warriors have to rest.
Drop your guard long enough
to know this place through your hand.
It has been the home of champions

and conquerors too – fearless, wild.
They left their stains of influence.
Language and customs bent to their rule,
but they have been ousted for good.

And what of future manoeuvres?
My belly is in the right place –
strategically located. Dream of places
your hand can go from here.

All other invaders are gone –
you are welcome and free to roam.
Your weapons will not be needed tonight.
Lay them down. Rest.

The Hero Tells a Story

The story came slowly
with pauses and little blurts.
Certain words separated themselves
from the general flow of speech
to stand out and be noticed.
Words like *naked* and *completely*
were picked out and left
throbbing under a strong red light.
Chinese and *older*, were also featured
in the story like water colour washes
adding tints of yellow and grey
between the bold black lines.

We wondered, while listening,
had he been too drunk?
Too startled by her tiny breasts
to see the curve from waist to hip?
Had he been too distracted
by her nipples to see her loosened hair?
Had he been confused, put off
by the boldness of her invitation?

'Take me,' she said, in English.
He recounted the story faithfully,
to that point and then started to
emphasise words which seemed
to us quite random and unfocussed.
Hotel, note, key, child, breakfast.
We imagined, without his ever saying so,
that he twisted her hair on his finger
and let his tongue loose on her chest.
Hair, finger, tongue, loose, chest.

Pleasing Students

The students want incense, flutes, chimes
and a digital video tape of her, teaching
in black pyjamas with white rolled up cuffs
in an oriental mountainous landscape.

The students want a tape of her voice,
'step left, heel down, shift weight, close hip,'
to play on their personal stereos, a voice-over
on top of the video musical sound-track.

The students want foot-print-maps for the floor
to show them where their feet should go –
Green prints for section one, red for section two
and arrows for north, south, east and west.

They want plumb-lines to hang from the ceiling
and spirit levels balanced on their heads.
They want small china cups of hot jasmine tea
and only good fortune in cookies.

So she did what her Chinese Grand Master did –
taught three healing sounds in the morning
and three healing sounds in the afternoon.
Then she buggered off to Liverpool.

Prayer Flags

There is so much the wind takes
as it takes these colour-drained
Tibetan prayers away.
They are supposed to go to heaven
but the path of the wind,
as I see it from the kitchen window,
seems to drag these tattered prayers

straight through the untrimmed privet
which divides me from my neighbours
and their three storey, leaking drain pipe.
I remind them again and again to fix it.
I can see their outside wall from here,
soiling itself toward a troublesome future.
But my neighbours stay inside too long

at weekends and know nothing
of the damage taking hold outside.
I fear my winded prayers might catch
on sodden surfaces of saturated bricks,
or my prayers may even seep
straight into my neighbours' flat
and never be answered or heard.

The wind persists regardless.
It pulls the tags of the wind chimes
so the clappers swing out to meet
long brass bars hanging in the cherry tree.
Then the blue glass rods begin
to tinkle in the budding dogwood
and bamboo sounds in the magnolia.

What a high achiever the wind has proved
itself to be in my little garden alone,
its power then multiplied by other gardens,
farms and even continents. These prayers,
fluttering like the flags of nations
riding the air-waves of the globe, chiming,
were certainly not caught next door.

When I said to the cop, 'Really,
you shouldn't be wearing shoes in here.
Would you mind taking them off?'
– he just looked at me.

Firmness, I thought, would work with cops,
so I dug my heels in and repeatedly jabbed
my mother-superior-finger at his shoes.
'This is a temple,' I said. 'Take them off.'

I was bare-footed, tip-toeing piously
across the polished maple floor
in a funnel of light from his torch.
I zigzagged to avoid big chunks of glass.

Oh! Another man wriggled in handcuffs,
wearing Doc Marten boots with such resolve,
I assumed he'd worn them from birth –
(hopeless, with handcuffs to undo the laces).

'Is this your place?' the cuffed guy asked,
not sounding sorry for the broken glass.
He'd managed to stuff his pockets already
with Chinese exercise balls and a Buddha.

Broken glass was strewn like cracked ice –
tiny scattered pucks on a sealed winter lake.
Some had kicked up on my black cushion,
studding it with crude rough-cut sequins.

I froze in my tracks, glass-shy.
Leaving my shoes at the entrance by habit
had always been correct. It was the way in –
into a sacred place, but not the only way in.

Job Description

Because I have dressed the king of Hungary
and know what a gusset is, please,
do not presume that a Greek God can come
out of this stitchery skill without effort.

Anyone can dress up and prance across
the stage in any of a number of guises.
It is not how we look or the costume we wear.
I thought you understood this by now.

You don't ask me to pour oil from a pitcher
at a great height above a small ordinary jar
the way the oil merchants of ancient China did
in the street, going from door to door.

Perhaps you think I don't have that skill.
You look at me and wonder what my other
talents might be. Singing, playing the lute?
Carpentry, archery, laying a lilac hedge?

You have no idea where the limit is
of what I can do. We are at the beginning.
The Chinese masters made it clear there was
nothing special about pouring the oil.

I do the things my job requires
and none of them is spectacular.
If you don't know what my job is,
everything I do astounds you.

Not the Sky

Not the sky
and not the rock pools
where the lichen is egg-yolk yellow
and not the sapling cherry tree
already showing promise of red satin bark
and not the water lilies in the loch
with stems as long as they need to be.

None of these things
will have to be remembered
as if they had been forgotten.
When I leave,
remembering will just go on
as it has always done.
Who would forget the sky?

The Martial Artist's Funeral

Thugs with flowers came.
There's no other way to put it.
You know, guys with thick necks,
leather coats and dreadlocks –
lads with tattoos, earrings, shaved heads –
bouncers with barrel chests
and arms which hung down,
gorilla-style, away from their bodies –
muscle-bound, their shoulders tight,
just plain bloody strong.

These hard men with flowers,
stood in the drizzle and talked
about the man they'd loved.
He had taught each one of them
how to let the punches pass.
It was simple really – block, then step aside.
These men together, damp from the rain
and the sweat of a thousand years of training,
put their flowers down and stepped straight in
before they lifted and shouldered the box.

III

Cut Fruit

Cutting fruit for you
as early and as quietly as I could,
I chose the only white plate there was
and laid the fruit out like a star.

I couldn't rest the plate on your back
in case you moved and tipped it,
so I held it above your left shoulder,
without moving, until you woke.

You pick a crescent slice of peach
and slip the juicy surfaces between your lips.
At once my tongue aches, my mouth floods.
I know I could suck the taste out of you.

Perhaps I'll have to get up earlier
and cut the pieces finer.
Dawn slides in an instant
and the juices have run in the plate.

Initiation

I set the table carefully this morning for two.
In the centre, I place the things we both can use –
the salt and pepper, butter and bread, the knife.

It is only breakfast, a simple ritual to bond us,
though another could tear us apart – old enemies,
trying to heal through food and acts of love.

Sometimes, the rituals make us belong
forever through pain to our traditions,
marking us with the scars of our ancestors.

I hold up the knife and both of us are crying.
It could destroy my Jewish face.
It could cut away your German tongue.

Sometimes, the rituals set us free
forever through pain from our traditions,
maiming the shapes we have come from.

You examine my features, those of any Jewess.
Your fingers trace my eyebrows, eyelids, nose,
then rest on my cheeks, afraid of bruising them.

I keep the knife in my hand, patiently
waiting until your hold slips from my face.
I drop the knife and you reach for it.

It is one of the tests set for us – to see the damage
in these faces, already flooded with tears
and survive, facing each other.

Night Vision

The bed is piled high with white.
All six plumped up pillows are white
and the night shirt I have on is white
and the lampshade and the blinds are white
and the rugs around the bed are white
and I wait here, covered, while you wash.
Then you come dripping, rubbing your rump
buffing your back, trailing the towel
and I open the duvet and draw you in
as the feathers fill their cases, freshness
from the bath, gardenia scent from the soap,
making much lighter the white in the room.
You tell me it's time to go to sleep,
but sleep is for people blinded by dark.

Big Blue Sofas

The big blue sofas are coming
early in the morning. We've cleared
everything out of the room
and made enough space in the hall.

You've had to tell me everything
quickly, before the doorbell rings.
When I felt your arm around me, I woke
to hear you say, 'My god, five bottles.'

The sofas are dark blue – navy, almost –
and one of them is as long as the wall.
The other one seats three people who agree
to sit up straight, or one person who sprawls.

You gather my breast from where
it has slid down along my ribcage
and then you find the nipple easily.
Some men have a knack for this.

The longer sofa seats four, which could be
three children and about two cats.
Not white cats, of course. Not white on navy,
though the people can wear whatever they like.

Even while gently scooping my breast
you talk about cocaine and smoking draw
and matted memories of greedy sex
as if I could absolve you, clear your slate.

The sofas will be set at right angles
to each other with a low table in between
on which everyone from both sofas can put
their feet and their remote controls.

I slide my hand down your back
further than most daytime friends might,
even though all night I had been careful
not to slip that hand between your legs.

One person will have to walk backwards,
I imagine, and the other one won't.
The cushions might still be wrapped
separately in thick milky polythene bags.

I want to love you on a new day,
clearly, using everything I've got
and I want to sit at right angles to the walls
and flip through every channel.

I can hardly wait for the doorbell to ring.
I want furniture to be carried down the hall.
I want big blue sofas and kids and cats
and cushions and perfect reception on the bloody TV.

The Dinner Kiss

The cooking had been a chore –
the knives not sharp enough,
no overall menu planned in my head
and the guests had not been counted.

Yet somehow everyone fitted in –
the Scots, big and boisterous, squeezed
beside the buttoned up Japanese
while the Americans brought in chairs.

Vegetables could have been the cause,
finally, of the seating plan's collapse.
The garlic scented potatoes with herbs
made everyone stand to help themselves.

I thought you were heading for the fridge
when you got up, the way an old friend can,
cool as you like, making mince meat
of the demure Japanese manners.

Maybe a can of beer or ketchup, I thought.
Just one of those sudden mid-meal needs.
And to tell the truth, there is nothing
I would have kept from you.

So, when you walked around the table
and lifted me out of my seat
as if your mouth had done it alone
without the help of your arms,

I rose, a stringless helium balloon,
so light, hovering over the table,
I thought I would never stop rising,
not ever, and then the kiss began.

An Embarrassment of Sunflowers

You burst into the garden party,
your arms so full of heavy-headed sunflowers,
that you probably wished at the last minute
they could have fitted behind your back,

completely hidden from our friends,
neat and tight as a bunch of spring violets.
You could have left violets in a teacup
beside my bed without saying anything.

But you staggered past the other guests,
breathless, dwarfed by your own extravagance,
drowned out by those loud-mouthed flowers,
paled by their blatant yellow.

You held them out in my direction
and I knew what they were for.
Everyone knew. They all watched, frozen,
dumbfounded as the music got louder.

Some of the petals stuck in my hair
and the stems were tougher than they looked,
cutting the palms of my hands,
not letting me simply snap off their heads.

The seed heads crunched beneath our feet
as we danced the blazing noonday dance,
the briefest dance there is, kindling
the lawn into flames, torching the sky with the sun.

Edinburgh, Late June

Tricked by the light afternoon,
we missed the hour to see the herbaceous border
in the Botanics in front of the giant hedge.
The beech leaves have already begun to darken
and the gates close at dusk.

Tricked by the light night,
we have missed the hour for restaurants
and need to wander further down Leith Walk
toward the harbour to find a chef
who watches the light and not the clock.

Tricked by the light morning,
we wake up every half hour
and search our hands around each other's bodies
looking for the answer to the question,
'Is the solstice really a time for love?'

Tricked by the light midday,
I forgot to write down your address
on the inside flap of the book you gave me,
but I remembered something else.
Light and love are not quite the same thing.

Close Range

I have a contract out on the word 'my'
although it never really did me wrong.
It never embarrassed me in public.
It never insulted any mother of mine.
I just want to take it out.

I could do it alone, with one of those
sawn-off rifles, fitted with a silencer,
sly enough for Main Street at high noon.
I wouldn't even need a telescopic sight
because I know I could get in very close.

This is not a back street vendetta, fermenting
over generations, but a sudden urge
to remember how it was before you were
my fella', *my* city-slicker's-dream-come-true,
my bucking-bronco-tamed-to-a-crumpet.

I liked the open space before I thought
of lassoes and corrals. You were just a cowboy
in the distance, riding across the prairie,
bareback, the sun steaming off your skin.
I was the city girl, a million miles away.

My, my, my, how fast a target can move
and line itself up in really tight spots.
I hope to God I don't miss
and take *you* out by mistake. You, *my* long-shot,
my tumble-weed-free-range-cowboy.

Phone Sex

I think we've got the wrong end of the stick.
One of us is supposed to unzip something
or at least make the sound of a zipper pulling,
or if not stripping, we are supposed to mention
some protruding little bit of us and say what kind
of garment is currently stretched across it.

We should be avoiding words which jar,
like suitcase, mistake, ticket, train
though, quite naively, you seem to think
you can talk me through this little episode
from the beginning right up to the end
and still manage to pull out just in time.

One Big Man

One big man dancing
is worth several skin–tight
scrawny ones who wiggle too much,
thinking thinness alone is a virtue.

Where does the idea come from
that dancing goes side to side,
up and down, back and forth, visibly,
like bones poking through a sausage skin?

Give me one big man dancing,
well–encased, he'll hardly move.
Nothing as crude as a foot off the floor.
Rooted, stuffed with shock waves.

Crossing the Street

Before he crossed the street
he must have spoken the words out loud
because they weren't part of a conversation.
I could hear the word coffee, the name of a café,
above the noise of the traffic before I saw him.
And then I saw him in front of me, asking
would I go for a cup of coffee with him.
He must have recognised me easily,
even after all the years our marriages took.
Did he think we could just carry on?

He might have stayed there, across the street,
shouting the names of all the women
he'd met, fallen for and fucked since then,
the names of diseases he'd suffered,
a list of all the countries he'd visited on holiday,
the dates and times of his children's births,
a list of the clubs his band had played,
all the names of the mountains he'd climbed,
their altitudes, their dates of conquest,
the cars he'd driven, the cash he had in the bank.

He might have stood there, across the street
waving his arms to get my attention,
then miming the scene of the death of his dog,
the later loss of his sanity, the pain in his chest,
the silent play-acting of the sound of his flute.
He might have danced on the pavement
of Threadneedle Street, in the heart of the City
in his pin-striped suit, as nimble as Fred Astaire.
He might have done cart wheels and back flips,
eaten fire, completely unnoticed by me.

But he walked across the street
straight toward me, his sentence in full flow,
making no attempt to bridge the years
with history or any hint of tenderness.
I thought he might have said my name
when he was close enough not to have to yell it.
He might have waited until whisper-distance
or said nothing at the distance of a touch.
Coffee, then. Yes, I agree. I need it. Yes.
Caffeine to wake me up. Right here. Right now.

Pillion

Because of (or in spite of) her short legs
she squeezed a little too much with her knees,
to keep from listing more than a bag of potatoes might.
He had told her to let her body go completely,
to let it match the tilt of the bike around curves.

Because of (or in spite of) the storm
she pulled her helmet down, letting the rain
drip off the tip of her nose right down his neck.
Too intent to notice, he zigzagged into puddles,
rutting through them, fanning sheets of spray.

Because of (or in spite of) his youth
she let her body mould itself against his back.
She could have held an independent posture –
upright, clear, keeping her large breasts back.
'What for?' she thought, giving in to his warmth.

Because of (or in spite of) her age
(she was a little bit older than his mother)
she wanted him to go faster on the down-hills
so she hooted instructions into his ear.
He couldn't hear a word she said, but he went faster.

Room in Large Family House

My son stops me wearing low cut dressing gowns,
sheer nighties with slits up the sides,
fitted, see-through blouses
or my bikini on the patio
in front of our new lodger.

Our new lodger is a hunk.
He walks around in singlets,
comes to breakfast in a barely tied robe
open to the waist, revealing a dagger tattoo.
My son never actually said, Mom, don't, but I didn't.

Not yet. In a few days my son will leave home.
He says he needs more room to manoeuvre.
Good. Then I'll have his room too.

Reviewing

I would prefer to have a love affair
with the man who wrote the good
review of my latest book of poems
than with the man who panned it.

I think this is a healthy attitude
toward sex as well as towards literature.

Found and Lost

I could say, 'you must have left it in the taxi'
or, 'let's phone the restaurant and ask'
or, 'because it was such a warm night
you might have left it outside on a bench'.

Then I could slip my bare arms into the sleeves
and feel the chill of the chunky brass zip
thud down, so cool between my breasts.
I could bend the fabric and roll back the cuffs.

I could sleep in your black denim jacket tonight,
and the next night and the next, breathing in
the scent of your skin, your hair, your after-shave
until your jacket starts to smell like me.

I could leave it in a taxi after that.

Kiss in the Dark

She has thickened around the middle
like a successful custard
on a wooden spoon.
Her face has grown square, strong.

Her legs are sturdy with veins
showing at the backs of her calves.
Firm, muscular thighs fold slightly
over her knees when she stands.

Skin blemishes, of course,
and bloating around the eyelids.
Her breasts begin to swell
half way down her chest.

She won't let her upper arms show
and wears sleeves even when it's hot.
A well chosen standing collar
detracts from her throat.

She loves you, nevertheless.
At arm's length, she ventures
a first caress in the dark.
Will you go on from there?

Formerly

Staying in the former wife's wing
of my very own former Scottish home
with you, my former English husband,
the father of my transatlantic children
is easy, since I know where everything is.
I can find the bathroom in the dark
and I know where the light switch is.
The china pattern pleases me as much
as it did the day I picked it out.
The pillows and quilts are tasteful too,
though I don't like the boot rack at all.
It's crammed with walking shoes and socks
I've never seen and dainty boots for hiking.
Correction. This is your former *wives'* wing.

Art in the Kitchen

for Joseph St. Amand, painter 1925-1992

I'll keep the floating eggplants in the kitchen
if I can remember to close the door.
Their frame is absolutely useless for holding them.
I suspected for some time they'd fly, but of course,
Joseph, you must have known it from the start.
Why else would you have painted them,
rising from that daisy saucer, edged in gold?

You've made it awkward for me.
It's never easy, saying to my friends,
'Please close the door. We're trying to keep
the eggplants from getting up the stairs.'
Some people don't mind, but some people do.
The word *door* is OK, but when I get to *eggplants*,
they'd rather it was cats or the smell of garlic.

A few people actually said so.
Mind you, it isn't just the eggplants
which are unstable. Do you see the woman
juggling in the painting over there,
held in a clip frame without any edges?
She's not exactly keeping in her place.
She tosses up a carrot a sock a strawberry a cat.

No one has complained about her yet.
As I see it, one problem is with vegetables –
any kind of vegetables depicted here in paint.
The blue black hides and hollow seeming insides,
the green stemmed party shapes, rising,
shiny balloons, not launched but simply let go.
No one is responsible. No one can be blamed.

The household flux is frenzied now –
worse since someone left the door ajar.
I know, my dearest Joseph, it was you.
Did you watch as the deep purple blimps
broke loose and slipped into the hall?
Did you follow them as they floated
toward the stairwell and rose?

A saner, plainer man might have
painted vegetables with gravity,
plates on tables, daisies glazed to China
and the kitchen would not be a place for art.
(Look, do you see the woman from the painting
standing on the table juggling?
Her feet are no longer touching the wood.)

Watch. She's beginning to float.
And that's the other problem, Joe.

Muscle Words

Yesterday I gave you *flex*
to put in your box of muscle words.
It was just right for the job.
Short, compact, English,
though bulging and rather proud.

Today I give you *extend*
and reach further than my body
toward you. I'm an acrobat.
The box will never be big enough,
to go beyond translations.

Boy with Canoe

He was behind the canoe in the shed,
testing a new look on his face
which he must have seen in a movie –
(maybe an old black and white one,
seen on a rainy Saturday morning)
and kept it ready, waiting for the day
he might know what it meant.

It started from the bottom of his face,
parting his lips, just a little.
It made his nostrils flare, but not much.
Then it spread up, flushing his cheeks,
but his eyes took the brunt of the burden.
They drowned in the backwash
of his own eyelids closing, opening.

She had come to check the paddles,
and thought no one was in the shed.
He heard the door and saw her come in.
Helmets hung overhead where she stood
beside life jackets and spray decks on hooks.
She chose a short, double bladed paddle
from the rack and butterflied it in the air.

In movies, at this point, the boy coughs
and the woman laughs, to put him at ease.
'I hadn't seen you there,' she might say.
and he would say, 'I'm sorry to startle you.'
But instead, they stared at each other
across the upturned canoe without
any desire at all for this kind of talk.

Dressing for the Stage

for Shan Otey

My teacher died last week. It was a blow.
I thought the news would get to you quite fast.
Frail and frayed, she died in San Francisco.

She taught me how to drape and cut and sew
fantastic clothes for any theatre cast.
My teacher died last week. By now you'll know.

She liked the bias, letting fabric flow
before she chalked a line and cut at last.
Frail and frayed, old seams in San Francisco.

Her face was lined, her hands were getting slow
from all the characters she'd known and dressed.
My teacher was theatrical, you know.

She could make anything – a walnut grow,
a river flow – a sorceress, unsurpassed,
unravelling, thread by thread in San Francisco.

Sewing wasn't it. It was the show
itself, the lights, the opening nights, the vast
arrays of roles to play. A seamstress? No.
Invisible, loose thread in San Francisco.

Apprentice

based on anthropology studies of how learning occurs in various cultures

A boy in Liberia with flexible limbs
and hand-stitched dreams
sits in the dust, cross-legged
while flies gather
in the wet corners of his eyes.
His head is tilted.
A jug of water spills
a cool splash on his foot.

He leans on the shoulder
of the master tailor,
barely watching the needle
pecking the cloth and dragging
the thread behind it,
as the tiny hidden stitches
settle themselves evenly.

His foot begins to twitch.
It knocks against a bolt of cloth
which doesn't fall.
A pole leans against the wall.
The sun presses on the village,
a hot iron, searing its back.
Seams open and lie down flat.
Gathered fabric gently curves.

The boy has nothing to ask.
He hears the scissors snipping,
and the blades of the shears slicing
a path through pale chalked lines.
Flat stones weight the cloth.

His eyes shut. The suits
have lives of their own,
dancing through the dust.
Their pure white cotton
shows not one speck of dirt.
The cloth, the cut, the stitch
drape on the dreams
he's always had.

They did find her, didn't they? she said and I said,
(because I had been taught from childhood
to tell the truth) I said, no.
They never found her.

Oh, never? she said, sitting up,
needing my help to arrange the pillows.
Oh yes, never. I remember now.
But what happened? she asked.
Why did she leave, where did she go?

To Cramond, I said. The foreshore –
to that muddy marsh, spreading
in front of the River Almond
where it feeds the Firth of Forth.

I forget how we knew that, she said.
Who told us, how did we know?
Remember the taxi? I said,
how the driver remembered clearly
the woman walking down to the water?

She went to the foreshore, he said.
I could see her in my rear view mirror,
heading straight for the water.
She had asked to be dropped at the Inn.

They do that sometimes, he said –
ask for the Inn but go straight to the water.
Why did she do that? my old friend asked
and reached for my hand.
I mentioned the note her daughter had left.

It said she wasn't coming back.
They did find her, didn't they? she said and I said,
(because I had been taught from childhood
to tell the truth) I said, no.

They never found her.
Oh yes, I remember now, she said,
lying back down on the bed.
She extended her arm enough to keep
on holding my hand for a while.

Flat in Philadelphia

I would have preferred
death for dinner table talk
instead of real estate
and your flat in Philadelphia
as big as the Ritz (only
one floor of the Ritz,
you said) and how to
avoid inheritance tax.

You're right. I'll need
a new accountant,
just before I die,
so I can put my affairs
in order and avoid
inflated death duties.
Property and tax are as
close as life and death.

Let's just suffer them,
together, stiff upper lips
still managing to chew
our food, clean our plates
and rest our knives and forks
together, pointing
in the same direction
at the end.

Character Reference

The boy next door is in court today
with our letters in his pocket.
Some of the letters didn't arrive until midnight.
They say he is honest, kind, wholesome.
He found a wallet once and gave it back.
His attendance at school was almost perfect.
He rescued a child from drowning in the canal.
He walked the dog and made an old man laugh
out loud to take his mind off dying.

We are his neighbours, we know him.
We actually know who he is –
the boy whose mother went to Canada,
the boy who supported his little sister,
the boy who had no food to eat
unless he carried it home in a rucksack –
white bread squashed beneath his trainers
as he cycled through Southern Cemetery
in the rain on dark Manchester afternoons.

Most of the letters tell lies about goodness.
The truth about goodness –
(well, it could cost him extra years –
just an ordinary, run-of-the-mill,
boy next door kind of kid
who used to leave his bike
lying on its side in the yard
across the back walk-way to his house)
would never have been enough.

Firewood

Cut and left where it lies
or hauled to your place and strewn,
or dumped in the yard and stacked.
Take your pick if you order wood.

Firewood stacked in neat rows
is the option selected by most folks
with wood-burning stoves who don't
go into the woods themselves.

They do their own stacking of course,
with pride, like making garden furniture,
features or walls and sturdy barricades
in the front yard, the side or the back.

We've just changed to stacked in rows
from cut and left and hauled and strewn.
The transition has transformed our yard
and boxed us in whenever we go out.

So we stay in, except to get the logs
and lug them to the fire when it gets cold.
Because the wood is stacked, we know
which log to get. We get the nearest one.

Cut, left, hauled, strewn, stacked
are the things woodcutters say
about wood. What I want to say is,
once the wood's inside, burn it.

Imperfect Birth Day

This sleeping baby wrapped in pink
could break the heart of any man –
destroy him. Who would ever think
this sleeping baby wrapped in pink
could push her father to the brink
of suicide? A daughter can.
This sleeping baby wrapped in pink
could break the heart of any man.

What to Do with Sorrow

Can I sing a short song to your sorrow?
I'll choose something with absolutely no sentiment
or, if you prefer, I'll just hum, or, I could tap
my fingers on the table in a light, lively rhythm
or, I could do just the middle-eight part of a folk song,
or something else bland. Really, a song might be nice.
Could I get it a coke, or a Ben and Jerry cone
or a cup of coffee or some taco chips?
Maybe just some water with ice?

I could take your sorrow out somewhere.
Maybe I could take it on a road trip with me,
if I could get a crash helmet to fit it.
I'd take it to the mountains on the back of my bike
and we could go camping, just for the weekend.
I've got a tent and we could drink cocoa
from tin mugs and tell each other stories,
really sad ones, by the campfire late at night.
I think your sorrow might like it a lot.
Sleeping in a tent and looking out through the flap
at the stars. Maybe even seeing a shooting star.
And I've got some of those self inflating sleeping mats
which make all the difference. They really do.

Maybe I could take your sorrow out, this afternoon.
I could take it swimming with me in the lake.
We could go on the bus so you wouldn't even need to drive us.
I could take my day pack with apples and soda and rope.
We could sun for a while and then make our way over the rocks
to the sandy part where we could splash near the shore.
Then we'd move out together and begin to swim laps.
Breast stroke and crawl, side stroke and back stroke,
and then go further out to the middle where the water's deep
and we'd smell the water while we swam.

Do you remember how the water smells?
a bit like mud and a bit like dying reeds
and plants and a bit like fallen petals of water lilies.
It smells like turtles and fish and water snakes
and bottoms of row boats and the wet wood of canoes
and it smells like the bugs that skate on it
and like everything that's rotting on the bottom.
You remember how the water smells.
Don't worry about us at all.
Your sorrow will be safe with me.
I don't think we'll be back early.
Go ahead and eat without us.

Snow and Forgiveness

in Britain, two ten-year-old boys murdered a two-year-old boy
in Norway, two six-year-old boys murdered a six-year-old girl

Perhaps snow made the difference –
how the blood looked on the snow,
slightly less rich as the pigment
must have seeped in through the crust
and left a thinner red behind.

Perhaps it was six years compared to ten.
Six-year-olds are supposed to play like puppies –
a bit too rough with the sole of a slipper
as they tear it apart, wagging their tails,
but older dogs should know to stop and heel.

Perhaps living in a vast open country
where glaciers have a part to play, moving
landscapes between what one person does
and what another does and what one feels
and what another feels free to yell in his face.

>   The Norwegian mother said
>   the children had played too hard
>   and we must help these boys through
>   the hell in their hearts they've made.

>   The British mother said
>   punish the boys harder and longer
>   until all hell freezes over –
>   we must seal them away for life.

The dead children looked like angels
in the news before anything had happened.
The British murderers looked like news
before there were any angels. God help us.
We are the dead and the freezing to death.

This and That, Now and Then

When I showed you this and that
we were together in the same room,
with mirrors all around us.
We saw so much of each other –
back and front at the same time.
I could put my hands directly on you –
sculpt the shape of your back,
guide your arms, adjust your hips
as you moved. I could feel for myself
exactly how warm your body was.

Now, I send you this and that
to read though I'm not sure if you do.
Even if my words move you,
I don't think they would show up
in your palms or your finger tips,
though I look for them just the same.
I shift your collar to check your neck.
I unbutton your cuffs and slip them up
in case stray letters cling to your wrists
or whole words show on your hands.

When I gave you this and that,
I loved the way we were together.
We didn't need to write things down
or plan ahead for blank spaces
when we wouldn't be able to remember.
Button your buttons. I can't read the words.
Put your palms on your face and press
the impression of what I wrote into your cheeks.
Seal the ink with hand heat. Remember
holding me. Glow red with the rouge.

One Woman Dancing

No, I didn't mind driving here alone
or walking in and buying myself a drink
or talking to young couples at the bar,
but to dance in this well defined cluster
of a few extra women takes guts.
It takes youthful rose-in-the-teeth abandon.
It takes middle age who-the-fuck-cares?
It takes knowing I'm-the-one-in-charge.

I don't have to dance if I don't want to dance,
but I do, so I do. One woman dancing.
Look, there's another. And another.
Each of us out there, eyes shut, rocking. Yes!